Joseph Sewell. A dark blue and white transfer-printed side plate, measurements unrecorded, of a horseman and castle. Note the repetition of the transfer, which was too small for the space to be filled. Mark M67.

MALING
AND OTHER TYNESIDE POTTERY

R. C. Bell
MB FRCS

Shire Publications Ltd

CONTENTS

Published in 2000 by Shire Publications Ltd, Cromwell House, Church Street, Princes Risborough, Buckinghamshire HP27 9AA, UK. Copyright © 1986 by R. C. Bell. First published 1986; reprinted 1991, 1995 and 2000. Shire Album 170. ISBN 0 85263 792 6.

Printed in Great Britain by CIT Printing Services Ltd, Press Buildings, Merlins Bridge, Haverfordwest, Pembrokeshire SA61 1XF.

British Library Cataloguing in Publication Data: Bell, R. C. Maling and other Tyneside pottery. — (Shire album; 170) 1. Pottery industry — England — Tyne and Wear — History I. Title 338.7'6666'094287 HD9612.7T. ISBN 0-85263-792-6.

ACKNOWLEDGEMENTS

The author wishes to acknowledge help from his earlier work, *Tyneside Pottery* (1971), in preparing this book, and inevitably the debt to the same individuals and institutions as acknowledged for that volume. In the intervening years more material and information has become available and there have been two exhibitions on Tyneside of Maling pottery, organised by Mrs Sally Madge and Mr Simon Cottle, making possible the correction of errors in the earlier volume and updating of information. The author is also grateful to Mr Christopher Waagepetersen, Keeper of the Kalundborg Og Omegns Museum in Denmark, for providing illustrations and for pointing out the strong ceramic link between his country and the north-east of England, and for providing the photographs on pages 16 and 21, and marks m73 and m74. The cover picture is reproduced by courtesy of Dorothy Anne Robinson.

NOTE

References in the text and captions to makers' marks refer to the number of the mark illustrated in the chapter 'Makers' marks'.

COVER: *A hexagonal jar, produced for Ringtons in 1929, and a Blue Chintz pattern jug produced for the same firm in 1935.*

BELOW: *C. T. Maling and Sons. Stampware, usually made by apprentices; unmarked but provenance known.*

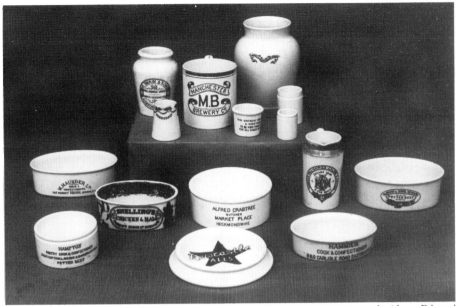

A selection of cream pots and meat-paste pots, ointment jars, a beer mug stamped with an Edward VII excise mark (between 1901 and 1910), an ash tray (m26) and a Deuchar's whisky water jug (m25). Rest m12 or unmarked but provenance known.

HISTORY OF THE MALING FACTORIES

The Maling family were Huguenot refugees who settled in Scarborough where William Maling was known as a wealthy gentleman. In 1743 one of his twelve children, also named William, bought the Woodhouse Estate at North Hylton near Sunderland. He founded the North Hylton Pot Works in 1762, using clay from a rich bed nearby, and appointed his two sons, Christopher Thompson Maling (1741-1810) and John Maling (1746-1823), to run the business. C. T. Maling was a brilliant young man who had a distinguished academic career at Cambridge. His brother John, in addition to his interest in the pottery, became a partner in a Sunderland banking house.

The firm began with the production of brown earthenware, soon followed by creamware and white pottery. Family tradition asserts that in the north-east of England transfer printing on pottery began in 1762 at North Hylton. The account books from the engravers' workshop of

Thomas Bewick and Ralph Beilby refer to orders from Maling for engraved copper plates between 1788 and 1798. Transfers from these plates were used to decorate their pottery.

In 1815 John's son Robert (1781-1863) transferred the business to Tyneside. Possibly the local clay deposits were becoming exhausted. The decision to move proved wise, and when the works at Ouseburn Bridge were built there was competition from only one other pottery in the immediate neighbourhood. The area was well established industrially and ideally situated for obtaining raw materials: coal and brown clay were mined locally, and other bulky materials could be imported cheaply in large quantities as ballast in colliers returning from the south of England.

The first kiln at the Ouseburn Bridge works was fired on 28th June 1817. Many of the copper plates and moulds used at North Hylton were transferred to New-

A bright blue and white transfer-printed side plate, 457 by 368 mm, with ancient ruined pillars in the foreground, and a lateen-rigged boat, an obelisk and a pyramid behind; marks M4 and m43. Probably made soon after 1853 when C. T. Maling took over from his father, Robert.

castle, and for a few years the products of the two factories were indistinguishable. Most of these early pieces were exported to the continent. The Tyneside potteries reached their zenith in the first half of the nineteenth century, and the Maling firm played a large part in the boom.

By 1850 Tyneside had become a renowned industrial area based on shipbuilding, engineering and coal. The rapid growth of the potteries in Staffordshire began to threaten those in north-east England, and several of the smaller firms closed at this time. Maling, however, benefited by the early introduction of mechanisation and was able to compete successfully with Midland and continental competitors.

In 1853 Christopher Thompson Maling (1824-1901) took over the running of the Ouseburn Bridge pottery from his father, Robert, and the firm prospered under the new leader's ability. Its expansion compared favourably with the largest of the potteries in Staffordshire. Special emphasis was placed on producing commercial wares — pots and containers of all shapes and sizes. By 1859 the two kilns at the Ouseburn Bridge works were unable to cope with the demand, and in that year a new pottery was built nearby on a 2 acre (0.8 ha) site known as the Ford pottery (later the Ford A pottery). The new factory was able to produce more in a week than the Ouseburn Bridge works had been able to make in a year. In its

LEFT: *Ointment jar and its plaster mould. Impress '1/4'; otherwise unmarked but provenance known.*
RIGHT: *White cream crock, 279 by 298 mm; mark M9; and a white ginger jar, 127 by 121 mm; mark m22 in green but without 'ENGLAND' beneath.*

(From left) Small white pouring bowl, 140 mm diameter, 76 mm deep; mark m40. A stewpot 241 mm diameter, 140 mm deep; marks M9 and m11. Large white pouring bowl 279 mm diameter, 127 mm deep; mark, black printed 'MADE IN ENGLAND' in two lines. No factory mark but provenance known.

(From left) A porcelain cup with a gold rim and monogram of the letters 'ACL', and beneath 'STANDARD SAMPLE'; mark m11. The cup was made elsewhere, probably in France, but decorated on Tyneside by Maling. A jelly mould, 235 mm diameter, 114 mm deep; mark m22 and impressed CC 11-12 (November 1912). A flower holder, 143 mm diameter, 38 mm high; mark m22.

(From left) A jelly mould 127 by 95 by 76 mm; mark M9 and impressed CC 9.05 (September 1905). A jelly mould 184 by 143 by 105 mm; mark M9 and impressed CC 906 (September 1906). A jelly mould 146 by 108 by 114 mm; mark M9 and impressed C 6.09 (June 1909). (Front) A white dish 181 by 137 by 38 mm; mark m22 but with 'ENGLAND' replaced by 'J. LYONS & Co LTD'.

(From left) A whiteware bulb bowl 241 by 191 by 83 mm; mark m23. A small whiteware meat dish and cover 279 by 216 by 79 mm, with the cover on; mark m23.

thirteen kilns the Ford pottery turned 80 tons of clay a month into some 750,000 articles. C. T. Maling amassed a fortune, mainly from the manufacture of jam and marmalade pots for James Keiller of Dundee, and later Frank Cooper of Oxford, together with dishes for potted meats and jars for ointments, medicaments and cream. Maling captured the market for the production of white pottery with transfer-printed trade labels and was a leader in the production of domestic white ware.

In 1863 Buckley wrote that 'Maling produced no first class goods ... but were responsible for supplying 90 per cent of the jars for jam makers in England and Scotland, together with exports to Denmark, Norway, Germany, the Mediterranean, and the British colonies'.

Much of the firm's profit was invested in the building of a huge new pottery half a mile (800 m) away on a 14 acre (5.7 ha) site at Walker. The new Ford B pottery was completed in 1878 and the buildings extended over 6½ acres (2.6 ha), the remaining areas being occupied by mills, workshops, kilns, warehouses, railway sidings and storage sheds. The Ford B pottery was reputed to be the largest in Britain, and, unlike most potteries, the main manufacturing processes were carried out under one roof.

For almost fifty years the two Ford potteries employed between them over a thousand workers. The Ford B pottery turned out over 1,500,000 articles a month. The Ford A pottery seems to have concentrated on making jam and marmalade pots, while Ford B dealt with the increasing demand for pharmacists' pots, photographic equipment and sanitary ware. The latter included bedpans, male and female urinals, inhalers and feeding cups, supplied to British and continental hospitals as well as for use in the home. Maling also produced 800,000 measuring mugs and jugs annually, which probably came from both factories, although it is difficult to distinguish between the products of the two factories. Sometimes an impressed A or B may indicate the source.

In 1889 C. T. Maling took his three sons, John (1858-1924), Christopher Thompson (1863-1934) and Frederick (1866-1937), into partnership, the firm becoming C. T. Maling and Sons. C. T. Maling died in 1901. The Maling workforce was predominantly female, with women operating machines and at times carrying heavy loads on their backs.

Skilled male employees made bricks for the kilns, moulds for pottery items and crates for packing wares for dispatch.

Parallel with the expanding commercial trade, decorated domestic services were produced in a variety of styles, reaching a peak about 1880. Some of the services had local names, such as Kilda, Blagdon, and Jesmond, whilst others were based on neo-classical or oriental designs. Maling responded to changes in fashion and was influenced by the Art Nouveau style, and later by Art Deco.

In the early twentieth century glass began to replace earthenware for commercial use, and demand for ceramic containers had dropped considerably by the early 1920s. The miners' strike of 1926 reduced the supply of coal to the two factories and the Ford A Pottery had to close in August and was never reopened. About the same time a slump in the ceramic trade in the United States, partly through the Wall Street crash, forced the Staffordshire potteries to dump their unsold exports on the home market.

In 1929 Maling began a long association with the Rington tea firm, producing for them an assortment of blue and white transfer-printed objects, many of which were sold at the customers' doors, filled with the company's tea. The designer of these pieces was Lucien Boullemier, who became Maling's art director in the early 1920s. Originally trained at Mintons in

A mochaware jug and mugs bearing official excise stamps of Edward VII; unmarked but provenance known.

(From left) A blue and white transfer-printed mug, 102 mm diameter, 127 mm tall, with one side showing the New Tyne, High Level and Swing bridges across the river; mark m31. A blue and white transfer-printed jug, 114 mm diameter, 171 mm tall, showing the Exhibition Buildings, Newcastle, 1929. On the other side are the bridges as seen on the mug, which also has the Exhibition Buildings on the side not seen in the photograph. Mark m25.

7

son, also named Lucien, who worked for Maling until the firm's closure in 1963.

Maling had a long tradition of producing commemorative wares, going back to the early years at North Hylton, and continuing to the coronation of Queen Elizabeth II in 1953.

During the 1930s production gradually dropped and the Maling family had to take out heavy mortgages on the assets to meet increasing running expenses. During the Second World War the government prohibited the manufacture of coloured ware for home use, white utility pottery alone being permitted; Maling held considerable stocks of decorated pottery which could not be sold and vital capital was frozen. Even more serious was the limitation this order placed on the training of apprentices, resulting in a shortage of skilled labour.

After the war production increased only slowly, and half the Ford B premises were used for purposes other than pottery. In 1947 the entire company was sold to Hoults Estates Limited, a firm of furniture removers. Frederick Hoult, its

TOP: *A multicoloured Art Deco plate, 286 mm diameter, decorated with a parrot, dragonfly and flowers; mark m27 and impressed mark 6.33 (June 1933, the date of the design).*
ABOVE: *A ceramic miniature of the keep of Newcastle Castle in a green-grey; mark m30 and above it 'MODEL OF THE OLD CASTLE BUILT — 1080 — FROM WHICH THE CITY OF NEWCASTLE DERIVES ITS NAME REBUILT — 1170 — LAST SIEGE — 1664 NORTH EAST COAST EXHIBITION MAY 1929'.*
RIGHT: *A souvenir plate, 216 mm diameter, with underglaze transfer print in brown, with a gold rim; (Above) the underside, m17 with 'MOSS,' replaced by 'LORD KITCHENER DRAWN AND PRINTED BY C. T. MALING & SONS NEWCASTLE-UPON-TYNE NOVEMBER, 1914'.*

LORD KITCHENER
DRAWN AND PRINTED BY
C. T. MALING & SONS,
NEWCASTLE-UPON-TYNE
NOVEMBER, 1914

Staffordshire, he was the son of Anton Boullemier, a designer who worked both for Sèvres in France and Mintons. Lucien produced many of Maling's best designs, including a plaque to commemorate the North-East Coast Industries Exhibition in 1929. Lucien Boullemier left the firm in 1936 and his place was taken by his

UPPER: *Two sides of a commemorative beaker for the Historical Pageant of Newcastle and the North, 20th to 25th July, 1931; mark m26.*

CENTRE: *(From left) Punch bowl, 292 mm diameter, 165 mm high, transfer-printed fruit and moss design number 32835 (1927); mark m25. Bulb bowl, 235 by 127 x 89 mm, with a blue-grey and white transfer-printed view of a Middle Eastern scene; mark m19 without 'REGISTRATION MARK' below the castle.*

LOWER: *A Hoults lustreware flower boat, 318 mm long by 95 mm wide by 64 mm high in the lowest part, 121 mm in the highest part; in pink, yellow and green; mark m33.*

chairman, took an active interest in the pottery side, and the name C. T. Maling and Sons was retained. He brought about a remarkable recovery, encouraging the designers to experiment with novel designs. Production rose, with at least half the output being exported. The installation of new equipment and the increasing experience and skill of the potters heralded a brighter future. Unfortunately Hoult's death in 1954 terminated the revival. Interest in the pottery faded, and gradually buildings were taken over for the storage of furniture. World competition increased steadily, the greatest threat coming from the Far East. Maling produced cups for the railways at one penny each, but Japanese factories, with government support, supplied the same article at a farthing each, including packing and transport charges. Japanese manufacturers also pirated English designs, Staffordshire as well as Maling, and in 1961 Maling lost their Australian and New Zealand markets to Japan. C. T. Maling and Sons closed in 1963. The equipment was sold and the buildings were converted to storing furniture.

FAR LEFT: *Smaller plate 194 mm diameter; Duchess pattern in blue and white; mark m17 (left, upper), with 'MOSS' replaced with 'DUCHESS Rd No 632985 MONSTER REGISTRERET MADE IN ENGLAND' in four lines. Larger plate 267 mm diameter; mark 26 (left, lower) but with 'DUCHESS' forming a third line beneath 'MADE IN ENGLAND'. The larger plate was probably made several years after the smaller.*

LEFT: *Deep blue on white transfer-printed cup and saucer in Two-man Willow pattern; on the cup the figures face right, and on the saucer left; mark m25.*
BELOW: *(From left) A white chamber pot, 229 mm diameter 140 mm height, with two narrow blue bands and a wide band of salmon pink; mark m22 but without the 'ENGLAND' beneath the castle, about 1918. This mark was used on many second quality pieces. A blue on white transfer-printed three-figure Willow pattern chamber pot with a gold lip; 229 mm diameter, 140 mm height; mark m17 but without 'MOSS'.*

ABOVE: *A multicoloured salad bowl, 216 mm diameter, 102 mm deep; in apple green, black, yellow, pink and purple; mark m26.*

ABOVE RIGHT: *A multicoloured ash tray, 102 by 102 mm. The recess is deep blue, lip red, yellow and green; mark m26.*

RIGHT: *A Hoults lustreware Peony Rose design salad bowl, 216 mm diameter, 89 mm deep, in pink, blue-green and yellow with a gold rim; mark m42.*

BELOW: *A blue and white Two-figure Willow pattern transfer-printed teacup and saucer and plate, the latter 133 mm diameter, with a gallon (4.5 litre) 'Jumbo' teapot, 267 mm high and 235 mm greatest diameter; tip of spout to back of handle 381 mm. Blue and white design. Tea set and teapot marks both m25, but on the plate is an additional impressed mark 12.28 (December 1928).*

Six multicoloured plates by Hoults; mark m40.

MALING DESIGNS

During the firm's two hundred year history more than forty marks were used, some being employed simultaneously. Popular patterns which remained in production for long periods may thus be found with a variety of marks. Dating of pieces is therefore only approximate, especially with objects made before 1920.

The earliest designs were not original and unique to Maling but were in a common British ceramic tradition. Throughout the nineteenth century Maling's transfer prints were based on popular patterns and as some of the firm's designers had been trained in Staffordshire this was reflected in their work. No marked pieces are known from the North Hylton pot works, though there are two tall creamware mugs in the Sunderland Museum which are believed to have been made at William Maling's factory. Some of the earliest products of the firm are thought to have been pink lustre wares on which printed transfers from engraved copper plates were applied.

The copper plates were transferred from North Hylton to Newcastle after the move to Tyneside and continued to be used for an indefinite period. A two-handled pink lustre mug with a transfer print known as Mother and Child is thought to be one of the first of Maling's Newcastle pieces, dating from the 1820s. The copper plate for this design is now in the Laing Art Gallery collection. The existence of copper plates illustrating the

Wear Bridge in Sunderland and the High Level Bridge in Newcastle and commemorating the Crimean War of 1854-6, suggests that an unmarked large pink lustre jug and frog mug decorated respectively with these designs were made at the Ouseburn Bridge pottery.

At least three varieties of the Willow pattern were produced by Maling: Standard Willow, Two-man Willow and Mandarin.

The Standard Willow is similar to the typical Willow pattern produced by the other north-east and Staffordshire firms, with three figures crossing a three-span bridge, a pagoda, fence, willow tree and two birds.

There are at least five variations of this pattern found on Maling pottery, with differing numbers of apples on the tree and variations in the position of the birds in relation to each other, and in the tightness and clarity of the print.

The Two-man Willow occurs in two forms. In the first, there are two men on a single-span bridge facing right, with a flat-topped willow tree on the left, a very large pagoda and numerous complex fences. Some examples have no border. In the second, the two men on a bridge

are facing left. The willow tree on the right has two branches on the left and one on the right. The borders consist of geometric, scroll, floral and insect motifs, which are known as the Broseley pattern, from examples made by the Caughley works near Broseley in Shropshire.

The Mandarin pattern, also known as Persian Blue, consists of a landscape with a lake and boat, pagodas and a willow tree leaning over the lake from the right. There is no bridge, and the rims of plates and bowls have a 'dagger' style border. The design seems to have been used for most of the nineteenth century and well into the twentieth.

The bulk of the domestic ware produced between 1850 and 1880 was decorated with either the Willow or the Mandarin pattern. In 1883 new transfer designs were introduced, together with new shapes for superior earthenware domestic services. Amongst these were the Kilda, Jesmond, Blagdon, Keswick and Portland. The Kilda, registered in 1888, consisted of a symmetrical design of interlacing leafy stems forming heart shapes around cinquefoil flowers, in Art Nouveau style. The Jesmond pattern was much heavier, composed of large leaves.

(From left) A square blue and white jar, 117 by 117 by 152 mm (lid an additional 38 mm) of Broseley and Two-man Willow pattern; mark m38. This is said to be the first piece made by Maling for Ringtons in 1928. A six-sided blue and white transfer-printed jar 133 mm diameter, 190 mm high, with great northern churches on the sides: Newcastle Cathedral, Selby Abbey, York Minster, Carlisle Cathedral, Ripon Cathedral and Hexham Abbey; the last is seen in the photograph. On the lid is Durham Cathedral. Mark m36. A square blue and white transfer-printed jug, Broseley pattern Two-man Willow with lid, 108 by 114 by 184 mm; mark m39. Inside the lid is a shield and 'RT' (Ringtons Tea), as in m38.

Keswick consisted of bunches of flowers interlinked by a bow ribbon. Above the bouquets of flowers is a dotted panel bordered by a pattern based on the *egg and dart* motif. These popular designs usually carried the title of the pattern in the trademark on the underside of the base, and the ware was given the name CETEM, derived from the initials of C. T. Maling. CETEM was described in a pattern book of about 1896 as 'A fine semi-porcelain body of brilliant appearance, strong and durable'. It was discontinued in 1931.

Among the oriental motifs was the Chang pattern with pagodas and scrolls, introduced in the late nineteenth century and continued throughout the first half of the twentieth. The Dragon pattern was another popular design, with a serpent-like form enveloping the exterior and the interior of a bowl. Originally printed in green, it later appeared in other colours; it was sometimes combined with different patterns and in the 1950s was printed in gold. Asiatic Pheasants portrayed birds strutting around an eastern landscape. A lustrous design introduced in 1930 in black, cream and gold in imitation of Chinese lacquer proved popular. In 1925 a pattern called Oriental appeared which was usually combined with Chang, but it lasted only three years.

TOP: *Polychrome blue lustreware bowl, 235 mm diameter, 64 mm deep; mark m25.*

ABOVE: *Polychrome blue lustreware box and spill holder; marks, box m25, holder m26.*

LEFT: *Two views of a modelled Urbino style vase, 406 mm high, 191 mm diameter, painted in blue, green, yellow and grey, recording the rescue of Andromache by Perseus from a sea monster; mark p41. This vase was one of six modelled by Norman Carling, Maling's last modeller, and painted by Lucien Boullemier Junior. It was made during the Second World War and used in a display area of the Ford B factory. This and a similar vase were sold together in 1995 for £5100.*

A bright blue and white trans-fer-printed oval plate, in Mandarin pattern (also known as Persian Blue); marks M9 and m67, with an impressed mark '1897'.

In 1928 Ringtons Limited, tea merchants, commissioned Maling to produce tea caddies. Orders for 75,000 or more specific articles were placed regularly. Rington items included tea caddies, teapots, coffee pots, jugs and flower vases. Some special patterns were produced for Ringtons. The items were packed with tea and, with a paper cover fitted over the top, were sold by Ringtons. Large deliveries were made before Christmas, and also for special occasions, amongst which was the North-east Coast Industries Exhibition in 1929.

The earliest known Ringtons piece dates from 1928 and is a square tea caddy and lid with a blue transfer print of the Two-man Willow pattern with a Broseley border. Maling supplied Ringtons in 1929 with hexagonal blue and white transfer-printed tea caddies, decorated with scenes of local bridges, cathedrals and castles, for the North-east Coast Industries Exhibition. The illustrations on the lids varied and included Windsor Castle, incongruous amongst the northern buildings. A few of the caddies had gilded edges, but these are now rare. The pieces specially commissioned by Ringtons include items decorated with the portraits of King George VI and Queen Elizabeth for their coronation in 1937. Beginning in 1953, Ringtons purchased items decorated in the colour called 'Victoria green'

combined with the Apple Blossom pattern. The rims were usually gilded. In March 1962 Ringtons ordered one hundred thousand Grecian jugs with a Godelia Spray design, but a few months later they terminated their contract with Maling.

Among the best known Maling pieces were their 'Jumbo' teapots made for retailers to put in their shop windows as advertisements. Only a limited number were made and they were decorated with a variety of Maling designs, the most popular being Willow pattern or Chintz. Another was Denon's Egypt, with two Europeans walking through an Egyptian landscape. Each teapot was accompanied by a proportionally large cup and saucer. One of these in the Laing Art Gallery collection is decorated with a cockerel, made about 1924.

Maling's wide range of popular floral designs, often with the name appearing in the trademark, included Orchard and Plum (1924), Wild Rose (1924), Irish Moss (1927), Japonica (1935), Tulip (1936), Columbine (1936), Fruit Lucerne (1936), Springtime (1950) and Blossom Time (1958). The firm's policy was to produce three new patterns a year, and these were used to decorate a variety of items. Most patterns were used for about four years before being withdrawn, but popular patterns selling well were re-

15

tained for much longer. Four background colours were used:- Victoria green (an apple colour), Japanese green (a dark green), ruby and pink.

Some designs were applied to ten or even more shapes, all of which would also be decorated with other standard designs. The permutations were considerable. In the 1930s the Flight pattern, portraying a flight of ducks, and Michaelmas Daisy were printed on a pink and blue background with additional gilt.

Maling supplied butchers' trays for the meat trade and pots for meat extracts. From 1873 to 1930 they made stoneware marmalade pots for James Keiller and Son Limited of Dundee, and in 1907 marmalade pots for Frank Cooper of Oxford in 1 pound (0.45kg) and 2 pound (0.91kg) sizes. In 1913 a 3 pound (1.36kg) pot was introduced and in 1922 five hundred 28 pound (12.7kg) pots were made as samples and sent to the United States. Stoneware covers were made for the pots from 1929. The Cooper order was cancelled in 1936.

Maling never produced porcelain but they imported French and German plain hard-paste pieces, which they then decorated. The original trademark was often concealed beneath a Maling castle, but traces of the original maker's mark may still be visible beneath. A few pieces in one such tea set have *LIMOGES FRANCE* visible beneath the castle. Such procelain appears to have been imported from about 1890 onwards.

Maling also supplied ware on a weekly basis to Townsends, a retail china shop in Northumberland Street, Newcastle upon Tyne. The wares were back-stamped with a Townsend mark, though sometimes there was an additional Maling one. The Cobblestone pattern was supplied to Ammacks of Leeds in three colours, green, brown or blue, and was used for a variety of kitchenware items, including mixing bowls, pantry jars, flour dredgers and rolling pins.

Commemorative ware mugs, beakers, caddies and plates were made in considerable quantities. Pieces survive made for the Silver Jubilee of Queen Victoria, as do some for the coronations of Edward VII, George V, Edward VIII (who was never crowned), George VI and Elizabeth II. In 1911 a thousand George V coronation mugs were made for Harrods in London and bear the Harrods trademark. Maling also commemorated local events, including the Newcastle Pageant of 1931, when one hundred beakers and five hundred square ash trays were produced.

From 1920 onwards the firm produced large amounts of lustreware. An attempt was made at the beginning of the twentieth century to reproduce the nineteenth-century pink tear-stained lustre, but with little success. Most of the Maling lustreware is modern in concept, using designs from the early 1930s. Many attractive effects were achieved by mixing a number of metallic oxides to produce a medley of colours. An outline transfer was applied to a biscuit-white item, which was then hand-painted and given a lustre glaze. Thus the same design may appear on a variety of differently lustred and painted objects.

Joseph Sewell. A pink lustreware cup and saucer; diameter of saucer 171 mm; cup diameter 121 mm, height 70 mm, mark M67. (In the Soro Amt Museum.)

Fell and Company. A bright blue and white transfer-printed serving dish, 279 by 241 by 64 mm, with two resting stags in the foreground and an ecclesiastical ruin behind; mark M48, but modified, there being no rope to the right of the anchor.

OTHER TYNESIDE POTTERY

Most Tyneside potteries were small and existed only for a few years; their pieces are scarce and therefore exciting finds for collectors. Only the potteries at St Peter's (Fell), St Anthony's (Sewell), North Shields (Carr), Sheriff Hill (Patterson) and Stepney (Turnbull, Wood) approached the Maling firms in importance. In the early days the highest quality pieces were made at St Anthony's and St Peter's.

T. FELL AND COMPANY

St Peter's pottery, North Shore, was built by Thomas Bell and Thomas Fell in 1817, trading as Thomas Fell and Company. Fell and Company manufactured all kinds of white, sponged, printed and enamelled wares for British and export markets. In 1869 Fell and Company became a limited liability company. The firm then produced mainly white and coloured domestic earthenware, with a small amount of lustreware. Under the limited company only printed pieces were marked, and these usually bear the full name *FELL & Co* although the abbreviation *TF & Co* was also used. See mark m65.

In 1862 T. Fell and Company exhibited at the International Exhibition in London, placing on show dinner ware, vases, table tops, lamps and chamberware.

The marks of this firm are difficult to date, but the earliest pieces made, between 1817 and 1830, are impressed with mark M44 or *FELL*. Later mark M48 was used, and in about 1840 the arms of Newcastle appeared in underglaze print with *FELL* or *F & Co* beneath. When the firm became a limited company in 1869 the mark was changed to *T F & Co*. The last reference to the firm in directories was in 1891.

SEWELL, AND SEWELL AND DONKIN

Joseph Sewell bought St Anthony's

ABOVE LEFT AND RIGHT: *Two views of a Fell and Company hand-painted lustreware jug, 140 mm diameter, 241 mm tall, in blue, green, red and gold with a gold rim, dated 1874; mark m65. The portrait is of Renforth, an outstanding Tyneside oarsman.*

RIGHT: *Fell and Company. A deep blue on white transfer-printed cheese platter, diameter 394 mm with a geometrical design; mark M48.*

RIGHT, LOWER: *Fell and Company. A pale blue and white transfer-printed plate, 165mm diameter. Marks: an incomplete and unrecorded impressed mark of a fouled anchor with a loop of rope on the left; also a previously unrecorded printed mark, m62, incorporating the name of the design 'CORINTH', a registration mark of 1845, and 'FELL & Co NEW-CASTLE' and the word 'IRONSTONE'.*

OPPOSITE, UPPER: *Fell and Company (Left) A multicoloured bowl, 216 mm diameter, 127 mm deep, in deep grey-green, plum, lemon yellow and light green with a gilded rim; dated 28th June 1829; mark M46. (Right) The interior of the same bowl.*

OPPOSITE, CENTRE LEFT: *Fell and Company. A blue and white transfer-printed Chinese scene on a side plate, 470 by 381 mm, mark M48.*

OPPOSITE, CENTRE RIGHT: *Fell and Company. A deep blue and white transfer-printed side plate, 413 by 330 mm in Wild Rose pattern. This name refers to the border. Mark M48.*

OPPOSITE, LOWER LEFT: *Fell and Company. A blue and white transfer-printed plate, 197 mm diameter, in Chinese Marine pattern; marks M44 and print mark 'CHINESE MARINE OPAQUE'.*

OPPOSITE, LOWER RIGHT: *Fell and Company. A bright blue and white transfer-printed soup plate, 260 mm diameter; mark M48.*

19

LEFT: *St Anthony's Pottery. A creamware plate, 114 mm diameter, with a filigree lip; mark M66. This is usually attributed to Joseph Sewell, though it may be earlier.*
RIGHT: *Sewell and Donkin. A small black and white transfer-printed saucer 146 mm diameter, of a boy, a girl and a dog; mark M70.*

pottery from Foster and Cutter about 1804 and manufactured earthenware, creamware, queen's ware and gold, silver and pink lustreware. Some of his pierced wicker baskets and filigree plates resembled those of Leeds, though the Tyneside pieces were heavier and of better colour.

Sewell carried on a flourishing trade with the continent, principally in pink lustreware jugs, ovoid in form with raised vine mouldings and cupids in relief. The best Tyneside lustreware was made by this firm and its successors Sewell and Donkin, and Sewell and Company. They also produced transfer-printed wares.

Dolls' tea services with diminutive teapots, cream jugs and cups and saucers were a speciality. Many of these sets have an attractive canary yellow colour with silver bands at the edges.

Sewell and Donkin succeeded Joseph Sewell in 1821 and carried on with the same products. In 1853 the firm is listed as Sewell and Company. It closed in 1878. Some of the stock seems to have been bought by J. Wood of the Stepney Pottery.

The Sewell firms traded considerably with the continent. From about 1820 to 1850 they provided creamware printed with Danish motifs. The designs were usually of buildings in Copenhagen or Elsinore but included scenes and portraits. They were printed in black or red

and were sometimes covered in pink lustre or had borders with black or another colour. They were usually tea or coffee sets and were used as ornaments on chests of drawers in village homes. Such pieces are rarely seen in England.

ST ANTHONY'S POTTERY (NIXON AND BOLAM)

A second St Anthony's pottery started in 1949 on a piece of waste ground at St Anthony's, from which the venture took its name. The proprietors, Nixon and Bolam, usually marked their wares in script *St Anthony's* (see mark p75). They began with local clay from a brickworks at Cowgate and later used imported ball clay from the Midlands.

In 1951 the firm moved to a large room over a garage in Argyl Street. The biscuit ware was painted with underglaze, and by overlapping a wide range of colours was obtained. Decorators carried out swift repetitive decoration by hand, each piece varying a little from its fellows, simulating studio work. The wares were then dipped in glaze and refired.

The firm produced jugs, vases, bowls and trays, an important line being mugs bearing children's names, which sold well. Other popular pieces were piggybanks and elephants turned on a wheel.

The firm went into voluntary liquidation in 1953. Their interesting work

Sewell and Donkin. A black on cream transfer-printed saucer, diameter 146 mm, with a scene of a small port and the caption 'HELSINGOERS HAVN'; mark M68. (In the Kalundborg Og Omegns Museum.)

Sewell and Donkin. Black transfer-printed designs of Copenhagen on a creamware cup and saucer; saucer, diameter 178 mm; cup, diameter 127 mm, height 83 mm; mark M68. (In the Soro Amt Museum.)

Sewell and Company. An octagonal deep blue on white transfer-printed Wild Rose pattern side plate, 343 by 273 mm; Mark m74. (In the Soro Amt Museum.)

ABOVE: *James Wallace and Company. A transfer-printed burial mug dated 10th November 1857, the last year of the firm; mark m78.*
UPPER LEFT: *St Anthony's Pottery (II). A hand-painted partly mass-produced leaf plate; mark p75.*
LOWER LEFT: *James Wallace and Company. A dark blue and white transfer-printed Willow pattern plate, 235 mm diameter; marks M79 and m77.*

should not be confused with that of the earlier St Anthony's pottery.

JAMES WALLACE, AND WALLACE AND COMPANY

This firm seems to have been started by Thomas Wallace in 1827 and is mentioned in a directory of that year, the address being Carr Hill, but a directory of 1837 gives the address as Forth Bank.

A directory of 1838 refers to Wallace, James and Company at 86 Blenheim Street, and this firm continued to be mentioned from 1838 until 1858, when the title changed to Wallace and Company.

THOMAS PATTERSON AND COMPANY, AND GEORGE PATTERSON

Thomas Patterson's pottery is mentioned in directories from 1827 to 1837. Sometimes the address is given as Tyne Pottery, Felling Shore, and sometimes as Tyne Pottery, Heworth Shore. This is the same establishment. A directory of 1847 gives Thomas Patterson as being at Sheriff Hill. Amongst the firm's products were pink lustre pieces with simple cot-

tage designs. See mark M83.

George Patterson may have been a successor to Thomas Patterson. The firm is mentioned in directories from 1851 until 1892 as being at the Sheriff Hill pottery. A directory of 1867-8 gives a second address of Three Indian Kings' Court, Quayside, which was probably an exporting depot. The directory of 1879 includes a description of his products: 'Patterson, G. (Manufacturer of C.C. sponged, painted and printed earthenware, all kinds of brown ware), Sheriff Hill Pottery'.

The firm produced lustreware plates and dolls' tea sets for children. They also made Willow pattern plates and dinner services.

JOHN WOOD AND COMPANY
Stepney Pottery, Ouseburn

This firm is mentioned in directories of 1877 to 1912. The directory of 1879 carried an advertisement: 'John Wood, Stepney Pottery, Newcastle-upon-Tyne, Manufacturer of white and coloured, and every description of brown earthenware. For home and export.' The directory of

Wallace and Company. A deep blue and white transfer-printed side plate, 457 by 368 mm, with two horses and a foal in front of a lake, with cattle and a ruined church in the background; mark M79.

1883 gives the address as 36 Stepney Street.

There is a blue and white printed dish in classical design in the Laing Art Gallery collection with the printed mark of J. Wood (m94), but with the impressed mark *SEWELLS*, suggesting that when Sewell and Company ceased trading in 1878 part at least of their stock of biscuit ware was purchased by John Wood, who then printed it with his own designs.

An advertisement in the directory of 1888 referred to 'J. Wood, Stepney Pottery, Manufacturer of every description of earthenware, also gas reflectors, and lamp tops'. In 1892 the firm became a limited company. The last entry, in 1912, is: 'Wood, J. & Co. Ltd. Stepney Bank'.

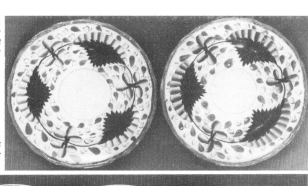

RIGHT: *George Patterson. A pair of lustreware plates in purple, green and brown with a pink border, 203 mm diameter; mark M85.*

BELOW: *George Patterson. Part of a transfer-printed doll's tea set in green and mauve; mark M85.*

LEFT: *George Patterson. A pale blue on white transfer-printed side plate, 330 by 267 mm, with a country scene of a woman with a child and a dog crossing a bridge. In the background are a waterwheel and three churches. Mark M85.*

RIGHT: *John Wood. A light blue and white transfer-printed soup plate, diameter 241 mm, with the Albion pattern; mark m93.*

JOHN CARR
Low Lights Pottery, North Shields

The Low Lights Pottery was established in 1814 by Nicholas Bird and passed about 1829 to Cornfoot, Colville and Company, which later became Cornfoot, Patton and Company. When Cornfoot retired and John Carr became a partner, the name was changed to Carr and Patton, and then Carr and Company. When the business became the property of John Carr, he and his sons carried it on as John Carr and Sons.

Originally brown and black wares were made, in addition to ordinary earthenware, but in 1856 these were discontinued and ordinary white earthenware in cream-coloured, printed, painted and lustred varieties was substituted. These goods were exported to the Mediterranean and to Alexandria for transport to Cairo, and by the Red Sea to Bombay and the Far East.

The firm's title changed several times, and the dates of the changes can help in dating a piece. In directories from 1844 to 1850 the title is given as 'Carr (J) & Co'. In 1855 the description is 'Carr, John & Son'; in 1858 to 1874-5 as 'Carr Brothers'; in 1887 as 'Carr (J) & Sons', and also as 'Carr Bros. & Carr'. There seem to have been two businesses at this time as in 1889-90 the description is 'Carr (John) & Sons, Potters and firebrick manufacturers'. In 1901-2 the entry reads 'Carr (John) & Sons, Firebrick manufacturers, 44 Low Lights', and in 1907-8 'John Carr & Sons Firebrick Manufacturers'. This seems to be the last directory reference to the firm, and pottery making appears to have been abandoned between 1890 and 1901, when the firm concentrated on firebrick production.

John Carr and John Patton were in partnership around 1844. Carr eventually took over the business at North Shields, and John Patton the Phoenix pottery at Ouseburn. John Carr and Sons manufactured earthenware for the home market and Mediterranean countries and made terracotta vases and similar articles for the building trade.

The stag's head impressed mark (M106) is said to be very rare, but this appears to be due to a high proportion of poor impressions, many being recognisable only by comparison with a well marked piece or by an accompanying printed mark.

ADAMS AND COMPANY (LATER LIMITED)
Scotswood-upon-Tyne

About 1840 a Mr Gibson started a brick and tile works at Scotswood-upon-Tyne, using local clay. In 1880 the works of W. C. Gibson and Company Limited were taken over by the twin Adams brothers, as Adams and Company, making sanitary ware with fireclay from a nearby clay pit.

24

ABOVE: *Carr and Patton. A dark blue transfer-printed cup and saucer, the latter 133 mm in diameter, with a young woman in the garden of a stately home carrying a parasol; mark m96.*

UPPER RIGHT: *John Carr and Sons. A pink lustreware tureen, 178 mm diameter, 140 mm high with the lid on; mark M106.*

CENTRE RIGHT: *John Carr and Sons. A light blue transfer-printed side plate, 406 by 318 mm, with a Mediterranean scene. A woman plays a mandolin to three companions in the foreground, while, behind, a gondola-like vessel approaches a neo-classical building of extraordinary design; marks M106 and m109.*

LOWER RIGHT: *John Wood. A brown slipware baking dish, 330 by 165 by 64 mm; mark M92.*

In 1904 Moses J. Adams began the manufacture of 'Adamesk' art pottery, using fireclay and decorated with leadless glazes. The large pieces were used as garden ornaments, bird baths, plant and fern pots and vases, cemetery urns and church baptismal fonts; smaller pieces were used in the home. A few pieces of Adamesk were unmarked, but most bear an impressed monogram *MJA* or *ADAMESK*.

Most of the feldspathic glazes used by the firm were invented by one of its employees, A. B. Searle. The colours were obtained by the addition of metallic salts, those of copper giving green, cobalt giving blue, titanium giving yellow, and manganese and copper giving bronze. The Adamesk pottery was fired in a muffle kiln at 1200 Celsius (2192 Fahrenheit), and the long period of heat produced subtle plays of colour not obtainable with the quicker tunnel kilns of today. The production of Adamesk pottery ceased with the outbreak of the First World War.

Alan H. Adams joined his father's firm in 1912 and became the director in 1921.

given as 16 Stepney Street, but after 1870 as 14 Stepney Street. This may mean a change of address, or possibly a re-numbering of the buildings in the street. Turnbull produced medium quality domestic wares, a popular line being an Albion pattern dinner service.

E. ROGERS
Railway Bridge Pottery, Ouseburn

E. Rogers is mentioned in a directory of 1857-8. He succeeded Morrow and Parke and was followed by William Blakey, who is recorded in a directory of 1858. Rogers enlarged the works considerably but only owned the pottery for a year or two. From the number of marked pieces surviving his output would appear to have been considerable during this time, or the marks may have been retained by his successor.

An impressed mark *ROGERS* was used by J. and G. Rogers of Longport, Staffordshire, from about 1784 to 1836, but the side plate and fish strainer illustrated seem to be of later manufacture and probably were made by the Newcastle firm.

JOSEPH BURN AND COMPANY
Stepney Bank Pottery, Newcastle

Mentioned in directories of 1852-60, Joseph Burn succeeded Thomas Bell and Company at the pottery which had originally been known as the New Pottery, Ouseburn, but was renamed the Stepney Bank Pottery about 1816. Burn was followed by John Charlton.

Burn used a Newcastle arms mark (m120) similar to that of Fell and Company (m54) in what appears to have been a deliberate attempt to pass off his products as those of the leading Tyneside firm of the period. Apart from the possible confusion in the marks, there is little of interest in this firm's mediocre products.

He was responsible for most of the firm's modelling and designed many of the shapes for the world-famous sanitary ware. He also created the unusual Elan pottery, and these pieces were impressed with his private mark *AHA* (M114). He also designed ornamental tiles, plaques and busts.

In 1975 the firm was placed in the hands of a receiver. Shortly afterwards the business was taken over by Jim Lee, a wealthy American, but about a year later the firm went into voluntary liquidation.

In 1977 Anderson Ceramics bought some of the equipment and moulds and the use of the name Adamsez. Adamsez (Anderson Ceramics Limited) has its premises at Dukesway, Team Valley Trading Estate, Low Fell, and still produces some of the Victorian sanitary ware of the original firm. They do not make Adamesk or Elan pottery.

G. R. TURNBULL
Stepney Street, Newcastle

The firm is mentioned in directories from 1863 to 1875. At first the address is

ABOVE: *G. R. Turnbull. A pale blue and white transfer-printed side plate, 495 by 419 mm, of Albion design; marks M115 and m116.*

RIGHT: *G. R. Turnbull. A pale blue and white transfer printed vegetable dish, 273 by 254 by 64 mm of the Albion pattern; marks M115 and m116.*

BELOW: *F. Rogers. A bright blue and white transfer-printed fish strainer, 368 by 268 mm, with a Middle Eastern scene of a camel, cattle and lake, trees, and an imposing gateway. Note the double crown pattern of the drainage holes. Mark M117.*

27

MAKERS' MARKS

Impressed marks are given a number with a capital M, for example M3. Printed marks are given a number with a small m, for example m2. Painted marks are given a number with a small p, for example p75.

Maling marks were used freely and at times haphazardly. Those recorded here are only representative, and the dates given approximate, based upon their use on dated items.

The word *Trademark* indicates a date after the Trademark Act of 1862, and usually after 1875. In 1891 the word *England* was incorporated into the maker's mark. From 1900 the words *Made in England* were added. Some Maling pieces have *England* and *Made in England* together, suggesting an earlier mark being brought up to date. Some Maling pottery has only the words *Made in England* and *England* impressed into the underside. Most of these were made between 1950 and 1963 when the firm was owned by Hoults.

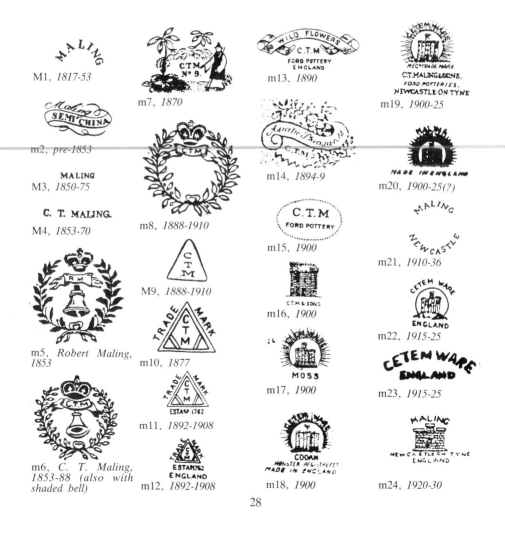

M1, *1817-53*

m2, *pre-1853*

MALING
M3, *1850-75*

C. T. MALING.
M4, *1853-70*

m5, *Robert Maling, 1853*

m6, *C. T. Maling, 1853-88 (also with shaded bell)*

m7, *1870*

m8, *1888-1910*

M9, *1888-1910*

m10, *1877*

m11, *1892-1908*

m12, *1892-1908*

m13, *1890*

m14, *1894-9*

C.T.M
FORD POTTERY
m15, *1900*

C.T.M & SONS
m16, *1900*

MOSS
m17, *1900*

COOAN
MONSTER REG STREET
MADE IN ENGLAND
m18, *1900*

RECᵒTRADE MARK
C.T.MALINGLSONS.
FORD POTTERIES.
NEWCASTLE·ON·TYNE
m19, *1900-25*

MADE IN ENGLAND
m20, *1900-25(?)*

m21, *1910-36*

CETEM WARE
ENGLAND
m22, *1915-25*

CETEM WARE
ENGLAND
m23, *1915-25*

MALING
NEW CASTLE ON TYNE
ENGLAND
m24, *1920-30*

28

m25, *1924-35*

m33, *1930-63*

m41, *1943*

M50, *1859-72*

m26, *1929-40*

m34, *1930*

PEONY ROSE

m42, *with pattern title, 1947-63*

DRAGON

THOˢ FELL & Cᵒ
NEWCASTLE ᴼᴺ TYNE
m51, *1824*

MALING

m27, *1929-63*

m35, *1930-55*

m43, *previously unrecorded*

m52, *1859-72*

m28, *1929-63*

m36, *1930-55*

M44, *1817-30*

m53, *1840-69*

m29, *1929-63*

m37, *1930-55*

FELL
M45, *1817-30*

m54, *1840-69*

m̀30, *1929 (also with castle and title in circle)*

TEA MERCHANTS
NEWCASTLE ᵁᴾᴼᴺ TYNE
m38, *previously unrecorded, 1930-55*

PORCELAINE
OPAQUE
FELL & Cᵒ
M46, *dated 1829*

m55, *1840-69*

m 31, *date unrecorded*

RINGTONS
LIMITED.
TEA MERCHANTS
NEWCASTLE ᵁᴾᴼᴺ TY
m39, *previously unrecorded, 1930-55*

FELL
M47, *1817-30*

m32, *1930*

MALING
MADE IN
ENGLAND
m40, *1930-55*

M48, *1830-40*

FELL
NEWCASTLE
M49, *1840*

m56, *1840-69*

m57, *1840-69*

m58, *previously unrecorded*

m59, *1867*

m60, *1869-90*

m65, *1877*

S^TANTHONY

M66, *pre-Sewell(?), 1804(?)*

SEWELL

M67, *1804-19*

M68, *Sewell and Donkin, dated 1845*

SEWELL & DONKIN

M69, *1821-52*

M70, *1821-52*

p75, *1949-55*

p76, *Mr Nixon's personal mark, 1949-55*

m77, *J. Wileman and Company(?), 1864-9*

m82, *previously unrecorded*

M83, *1821-7*

M84, *Thomas Patterson(?), 1837-47*

M85, *1837-47*

G PATTERSON

GATESHEAD ON TYNE

M86, *1851-92*

M71, *1821-52*

M72, *1853-78*

M73, *previously unrecorded, post - 1852(?)*

M74, *previously unrecorded, c 1853-78*

m78, *dated 1857*

WALLACE·&·Co

M79, *1858-92*

m80, *1858-92*

m87, *1851-92*

m88, *1851-92*

m89, *1851-92*

m90, *1851-92*

m61, *with registration mark of 1845*

m62, *previously unrecorded*

m63, *1869-90*

m64, *1869-90*

m81, *1858-92*

**J. WOOD
NEWCASTLE**

M91, *1872-1910*

*Stepney Pottery
Newcastle upon Tyne*

Fire Proof

M92, *1879-1910*

m93, *1879-1910*

m94, *1879-1910*

m95, *J. Wood, 1879-1910*

m96, *previously unrecorded*

M97, *c 1844-50*

m98, *c 1844-50*

m99, *c 1844-50*

m100, *1844-50*

m101, *1844-50*

PORCELAINE
OPAQUE
J. CARR & SON

m102, *1855-8*

m103, *1855-8*

JOHN CARR & SONS
NORTH
SHIELDS

M104, *1887-1900*

m105, *1887-1900*

M106, *1887-1900*

m107, *1887-1900*

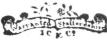

M108, *1855-8*

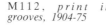

m109, *previously unrecorded, 1887-1900*

M110, *Moses J. Adams, 1904-14*

"ADAMESK"

M111, *1904-75*

"ADAMESK"

M112, *print in grooves, 1904-75*

M113, *1912-75*

M114, *Alan H. Adams, 1912-75*

TURNBULL
STEPNEY

M115, *1863-6*

m116, *previously unrecorded, 1863-6*

ROGERS

M117, *1857-60*

M118, *1852-60*

m119, *Burn and Company, 1852-60*

31

FURTHER READING

Bell, R. C. *Tyneside Pottery*. Studio Vista, 1971.

Bell, R. C., and Gill, M. A. V. *The Potteries of Tyneside*. Frank Graham, Newcastle, 1973.

Bell, R. C.; Dixon, L., and Cottle, S. H. *Maling, A Tyneside Pottery*. Tyne and Wear County Council Museums, 1981.

Buckley, F. 'Potteries on the Tyne and Other Northern Potteries during the Eighteenth Century' in *Archaeologia Aeliana*, Fourth Series, 1929, pages 68-82.

Chaffers, W. *Marks and Monograms on European and Oriental Pottery and Porcelain*. Reeves & Turner, London, 1891.

Gill, M. A. V. 'The Potteries of Tyne and Wear, and Their Dealings with the Beilby/Bewick Workshop' in *Archaeologia Aeliana*, Fifth Series, Volume IV, 1976, pages 151-70.

Gray, D. K. *Introduction to Maling*. Webb & Sons Pty Ltd, Adelaide, South Australia, undated but *c.*1985.

Jewitt, L. *The Ceramic Art of Great Britain*. J. S. Virtue & Company, London, 1882.

Litchfield, F. *Pottery and Porcelain*. Truslove & Hanson, New York, 1905.

Moore, S., and Ross, C. *Maling, The Trademark of Excellence!* Tyne and Wear Museum Services, 1989.

Shaw, J. T. *The Potteries of Wearside*. Sunderland Public Libraries, Museum and Art Gallery, fourth edition 1973.

PLACES TO VISIT

The following museums have good collections of Tyneside pottery. Intending visitors are advised to find out the times of opening before making a special journey.

GREAT BRITAIN
Laing Art Gallery, Newbridge Street, Newcastle upon Tyne NE1 8AG. Telephone: 0191 232 7734.

Shipley Art Gallery, Prince Consort Road, Gateshead, Tyne and Wear NE8 4JB. Telephone: 0191 477 1495.

DENMARK
Lolland-Falsters Stiftsmuseums, 22 Jernbanegade, 4930 Maribo, Lolland.

F. Rogers. A bright blue and white transfer-printed Willow pattern side plate, 610 by 394 mm; mark M117.